Rebecca York Hanlon   Jake Kimball

PEARSON
Longman

My Family

1. **Listen and repeat.**

1. My father is taller than my mother.

2. My sister's hair is curlier than my brother's hair.

3. My uncle is more nervous than my aunt.

4. My cousin Ana's grades are better than my cousin Maria's grades.

5. My grandfather is the oldest person in the family.

6. My grandmother is the friendliest person in the family.

7. My big sister is the most beautiful person of all.

8. My cousin David is the worst soccer player in the family.

Let me tell you about my family.

2.  **Describe the picture.**

3. **Listen and repeat. Role-play.**

4. **Listen. Sing or chant.**

Family Vacation Photos

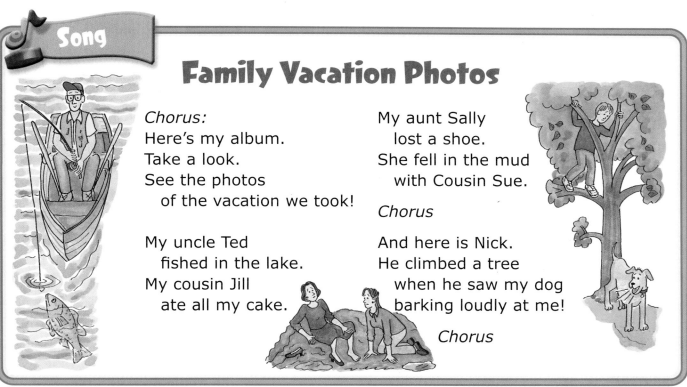

Chorus:
Here's my album.
Take a look.
See the photos
  of the vacation we took!

My uncle Ted
  fished in the lake.
My cousin Jill
  ate all my cake.

My aunt Sally
  lost a shoe.
She fell in the mud
  with Cousin Sue.

Chorus

And here is Nick.
He climbed a tree
  when he saw my dog
  barking loudly at me!

Chorus

5. ^{A6} **Listen and repeat.**

My father is taller than my mother.

short → shorter than	big → bigger than	easy → easier than
young → younger than	thin → thinner than	curly → curlier than

My uncle is more nervous than my aunt.

nervous → more nervous than   intelligent → more intelligent than

My cousin Ana's grades are better than my cousin Maria's grades.

good → better than   bad → worse than

6. Write.

Aunt Jenny / Aunt Rosa   Sam / little brother Louis   Uncle Tim / Uncle Bob   Cousin Ken / Cousin Pat

1. (short)   Aunt Jenny <u>is shorter than Aunt Rosa</u>.

2. (thin)   Aunt Rosa _____.

3. (young)   Louis _____.

4. (tall)   Sam _____.

5. (nervous)   Uncle Tim _____.

6. (curly)   Uncle Bob's hair _____.

7. (good)   Cousin Ken's pie _____.

8. (bad)   Cousin Pat's pie _____.

9. (intelligent)   Uncle Bob _____.

the -est
the most
the best, the worst

7. Listen and repeat.

My grandfather is **the oldest** person in my family.

old → the oldest	big → the biggest	easy → the easiest
rich → the richest	thin → the thinnest	pretty → the prettiest

My big sister is **the most** beautiful girl of all.

beautiful → the most beautiful   intelligent → the most intelligent
exciting → the most exciting   interesting → the most interesting
expensive → the most expensive   nervous → the most nervous

My cousin David is **the worst** soccer player in my family.

good → the best   bad → the worst

8. Complete the sentences.

My grandmother Alicia is (1) (old) _____the oldest_____ person in my family. She is (2) (rich) _____ person, too. Her house is (3) (big) _____ and (4) (beautiful) _____ of all our houses. Her car is (5) (new) _____ and (6) (expensive) _____. She wears (7) (good) _____ clothes and goes on (8) (exciting) _____ vacations. She is also (9) (interesting) _____ person I know!

9. What about your family? Listen and write.

1. _My mother is the most intelligent person in my family._

2. _____

3. _____

4. _____

5. _____

She watched TV last night.
She didn't read a book yesterday.

10. A9 **Listen and repeat.**

My uncle Pedro walked to our house last week.

walk → walked   study → studied   close → closed
listen → listened   try → tried   taste → tasted

My uncle Pedro didn't walk to our house yesterday.

didn't walk   didn't study   didn't close
didn't listen   didn't cry   didn't taste

11. Write the past tense form for each verb.

1. watch _____   5. glue _____

2. cry _____   6. talk _____

3. laugh _____   7. smell _____

4. visit _____   8. jump _____

12. Complete the sentences.

Cousin Alex (1) (visit) _____visited_____ us last Saturday. We (2) (play/neg.)

_____ outside, but we had fun. My sister Claudia (3) (share) _____

her toys and games with us. We (4) (help) _____ her make some cookies.

Then we (5) (watch) _____ TV. The cookies (6) (smell) _____

delicious, but we (7) (taste/neg.) _____ them. They were too hot. We

(8) (laugh) _____ and (9) (talk) _____ all afternoon.

13. **Listen and repeat.**

Uncle Ted caught a big fish yesterday.

He put it on the kitchen table.

catch → caught   eat → ate   put → put
read → read   sing → sang   write → wrote

Uncle Ted didn't catch a lot of fish.

didn't catch   didn't eat   didn't put
didn't read   didn't sing   didn't write

4. Write the past tense form of each verb.

1. buy _____   4. eat _____   7. see _____

2. do _____   5. go _____   8. take _____

3. drink _____   6. make _____

5. What did you do last weekend? Write.

1. I went to the beach with my cousin.

2. _____

3. _____

4. _____

5. _____

Writing

16. Read.

The Descriptive Paragraph

A descriptive paragraph has one main idea. Adjectives give details about that idea. They help to make a picture in a reader's mind.

17. Write the words in the correct column or columns.

| bad | cloudy | delicious | hard | loud |
| noisy | pretty | soft | sour | sweet |

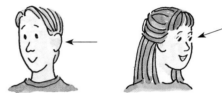 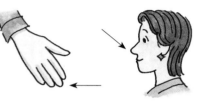

Hear	See	Touch	Smell	Taste

18. Write sentences. Use the words in 17.

1. _The music on the radio was very loud._

2. _____

3. _____

4. _____

5. _____

6. _____

 Unit 1

Writing

9. Read Julia's paragraph about a family party.

Last night, my family had a party for my father's birthday. The weather was nice and cool. We put long tables under the trees. We put pretty lights in the tallest trees. We put white tablecloths and red candles on the tables. There were delicious desserts, but the birthday cake was the best dessert of all. After dinner, my uncles played their guitars and we sang songs. We danced, told funny stories, and laughed. It was the most exciting party ever!

10. Write eight adjectives that help you "see" Julia's party.

_____ _____ _____ _____

_____ _____ _____ _____

11. Write a descriptive paragraph about a family party.

22. 💬 **Play and say.**

bad	beautiful	big	expensive	good	intelligent
new	old	rich	short	young	

> The rose is more beautiful than the other plant.

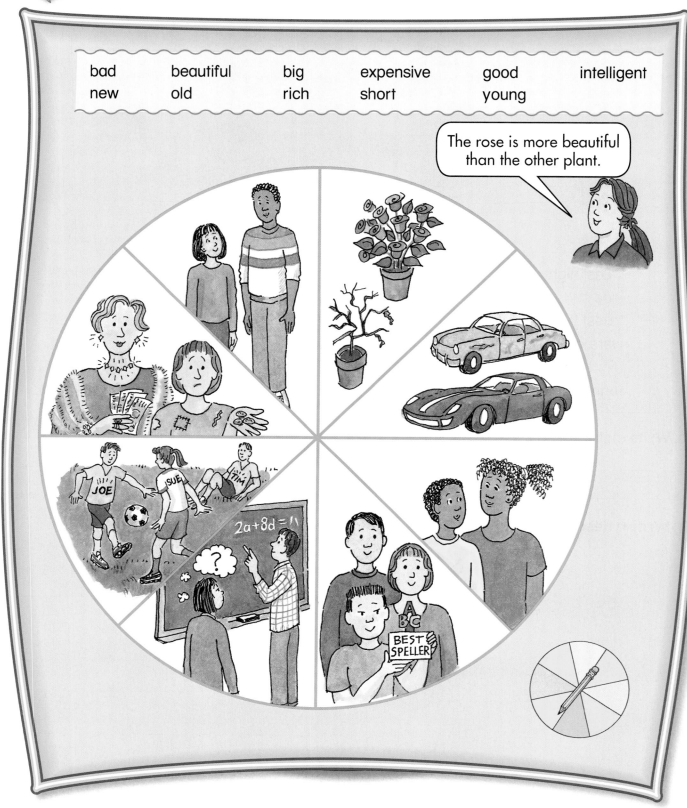

23. Read and discuss.

Appreciate Time with Family

You can learn family stories from your older relatives.

You can be a role model for younger members of your family.

24. Discuss the questions. Write.

1. Why is it important to know your family history?

_____

2. How can you help your family?

_____

Work and Play Every Day

1. 🎵 A17 **Listen and repeat.**

1. Betty helps with breakfast every morning.

2. She sweeps the floor every day.

3. She and her friends ride their bikes every day after school.

4. She and her friends go to the movies on the weekend.

5. Paul feeds the cat and walks the dog every morning.

6. He takes out the garbage every day.

7. He and his friends go skateboarding every afternoon.

8. He and his friend play video games on the weekend.

2. 💬 **Describe the pictures.**

3. **Listen and repeat. Role-play.**

4. **Listen. Sing or chant.**

Song

Seven Days

Monday through Friday
  there's nothing new.
I always know what
  I'm going to do.
La la la . . .

I get up at seven
  and sweep the floor,
  eat breakfast, get dressed,
  and go out the door.
La la la . . .

At four I do homework,
  then ride my bike.
I skateboard with friends
  or play games I like.
La la la . . .

Saturday and Sunday,
  I rest and relax.
I always have fun,
  and those are the facts!
La la la . . .

Work and Play Every Day

5.  **Listen and repeat.**

I play chess every day.
My brother plays chess once a week.
My parents play chess once a month.

6. Complete the sentences.

1. (take)   I _____take_____ out the garbage every day.

2. (make) Sue and Ben _____ dinner at 6:00 P.M.

3. (feed)   Mariko _____ her cat once a day.

4. (go)   We _____ to the movies on the weekend.

5. (do)   Sam _____ his homework at 7:00 P.M.

6. (ride)   Gloria _____ her bike every day.

7. (listen) I always _____ to music at bedtime.

8. (go)   Jaehak _____ skateboarding on the weekend.

7. Write about your own activities.

1. _____

2. _____

3. _____

4. _____

8. 💬 **Talk about your family's activities.**

My father works five
days a week, and
sometimes on Saturday.

My dad goes to
soccer games on
Saturday.

always, sometimes, usually, never
every day, once a month,
on the weekend, twice a year

A15

. **Listen and repeat.**

I always do my homework.
My mother sometimes plays piano.

I exercise every day.
Jack washes the car once a month.

They usually walk to school.
My sister never plays video games.

Sue watches baseball on the weekend.
Mario visits Argentina twice a year.

0. **Say. Use *always*, *never*, *sometimes*, or *usually*.**

Pam	Sunday	Monday	Tuesday	Wednesday	Thursday	Friday	Saturday
gets up at 7:00			✓		✓		
eats her vegetables	✓	✓	✓	✓	✓	✓	✓
goes hiking							
takes out the trash	✓		✓		✓		✓

1. **Write. Use *every day*, *on the weekend*, *once a week*, or *three times a week*.**

Jaehak	Sunday	Monday	Tuesday	Wednesday	Thursday	Friday	Saturday
brushes his teeth	✓	✓	✓	✓	✓	✓	✓
plays baseball				✓			
walks to school		✓	✓		✓		
makes his bed	✓						✓

1. _____

2. _____

3. _____

4. _____

12.  **Listen and repeat.**

I'm going to do my homework. → I'm not going to watch TV.
Maria's going to make cookies. → She isn't going to make a cake.
We're going to go swimming. → We aren't going to play tennis.
They're going to ride their bikes. → They aren't going to walk home.

13. Look. Combine and write sentences.

Verb *be*	*going to*	Action Verb
am		play video games
		go to the movies
is	going to	clean his room
		take photographs
are		play basketball
		make my bed

1. (I)   I'm going to play video games.

2. (He) _____

3. (We) _____

4. (They) _____

5. (I) _____

6. (She) _____

14. Ask and answer. **What is David going to do? What is he not going to do?**

15. Write sentences. Use _usually_ and _today_.

Usually   Today

1. <u>Paul usually goes skateboarding, but today he's going to</u> <u>ride his bike.</u>

2. _____

_____

3. _____

_____

4. _____

_____

16. What are you going to do this weekend? What are you not going to do? Write.

1. <u>I'm going to visit my cousins.</u>

2. <u>I'm not going to ride my bike.</u>

3. _____

4. _____

5. _____

6. _____

7. _____

8. _____

9. _____

10. _____

Writing

17. Read.

Parts of a Paragraph

A paragraph can have a title.

A paragraph has a topic sentence that describes the main idea. It is usually the first sentence.

A paragraph has detail sentences that give more information about the main idea.

A paragraph can have a closing sentence. It usually describes the main idea in different words.

18. Read Lisa's paragraph. Identify the parts of the paragraph.

closing sentence   detail sentences
title   topic sentence

I Love Weekends } (1)

by Lisa Brown

(2)

Weekends with my grandmother are wonderful. On Saturdays, I always help my grandmother make lunch. After lunch, we usually work in the garden. I choose the flowers, and my grandmother plants them in the ground. In the afternoon, we like to listen to music or read. On Sundays, my grandmother and I usually go to the park. We watch the boats on the water, or we sit under the trees. On the way home, we sometimes buy ice cream. } (3) I love to spend weekends with my grandmother!

(4)

1. _____

2. _____

3. _____

4. _____

19. Read Lisa's paragraph again. Think about your weekends. What do you usually do? Make a list.

Lisa	You
helps grandmother make lunch	
works in the garden	
listens to music	
reads	
goes to the park	
buys ice cream	

20. Write a paragraph about your weekends. Write a title, a topic sentence, detail sentences, and a closing sentence.

_____
title

by _____
name

_____

_____

_____

_____

_____

_____

_____

_____

_____

21. 💬 **Play and say.**

What are you going to do today?

 I'm going to play soccer.

22. 🗨 **Read and discuss.**

Balance Work and Play

Plan your time and do your work every day.

Plan some time to play or relax every day.

23. 🗨 **Discuss the questions. Write.**

. Why is it important to plan your time?

_____

. Do you work too much? Do you play too much?

_____

Family History Detective

How much do you know about your family's history? Do you know where your relatives lived long ago? Do you know the name of your grandfather's mother? Learning about these relatives (or *ancestors*) can be very exciting. There are many ways to find information about your ancestors. And guess what? Your own home is a good place to start!

Talk to your parents, grandparents, and cousins about family members they remember. Write down the names of these ancestors. Find out as much as you can about when your ancestors were born, where they lived, and how many children they had. You may want to begin a family tree. (A *family tree* is a diagram that shows family generations over time.)

In your home, you can look for written information about family births, deaths, and marriages. Old photos, family Bibles, letters, and diaries may have valuable information about your ancestors. Look in the attic, the basement, old boxes, and desk drawers. You never know where you might find clues to your family's history. So be a family history detective and find out what you can about members of your family who lived long ago!

Vacation Days

1. **Listen and repeat.**

Starfish Beach is as crowded as Seahorse Beach.

The Starfish Hotel is as popular as the Seahorse Hotel.

Seahorse Beach isn't as clean as Starfish Beach.

The sand at Seahorse Beach isn't as soft as the sand at Starfish Beach.

Starfish Beach isn't as exciting as Seahorse Beach.

The Seahorse Hotel isn't as new as the Starfish Hotel.

2. **Describe the pictures.**

A19 Listen and repeat. Role-play.

① Do you want to try snowboarding later?

② Not me. It's more dangerous than skiing.

③ Well, I think skiing is as dangerous as snowboarding!

④ Let's ride sleds. I have mine here. It's fun and fast.

A20 Listen. Sing or chant.

Song

My Dream Vacation

I'd like to visit Turkey
    and then go on to Spain.
I'd like to visit Mexico.
I hope it doesn't rain!

I'd like to climb a pyramid.
It really sounds like fun!
I'd travel through the desert
    to see the sand and sun.

I'd like to see Korea
    and visit China's wall,
or take a boat ride up the Nile
or see a waterfall.

I'd like to take some photos
    and buy some souvenirs.
I'd like to make new friends
    to keep for many years!

5. Listen and repeat.

crowded

Starfish Beach is crowded today.
Starfish Beach was crowded yesterday.
Starfish Beach is as crowded as it was yesterday.

heavy

My suitcase is heavy.
Your suitcase is heavy.
My suitcase is as heavy as your suitcase.

6. Complete the sentences.

1. (nice)   Today's weather is _____as nice as_____ yesterday's weather.

2. (good)   The hotel café is _____ the Star Café.

3. (warm)   The water is _____ it was yesterday.

4. (expensive) Our plane tickets were _____ your tickets.

5. (friendly)   Ricky is _____ Maya.

6. (clean)   Our beach is _____ White Sand Beach.

7. Point and say.

Julia /
funny /
Mary

Kim's
camera /
expensive /
Bob's
camera

Grace /
intelligent /
Peter

Ellen /
tall /
Barbara

Today's
homework /
difficult /
yesterday's
homework

The sand /
hot /
it was
yesterday

Unit 3

 **Listen and repeat.**

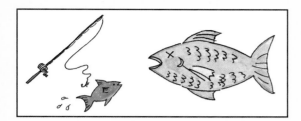

My fish isn't as big as your fish.
Your fish is bigger.

Kate's hair isn't as curly as Meg's hair.
Meg's hair is curlier.

Talk about Coco Beach and Sandy Point Beach.

clean   crowded   good   popular   pretty   soft

Coco Beach isn't as clean as Sandy Point Beach.

Yes, Sandy Point Beach is cleaner than Coco Beach.

Coco Beach

Sandy Point Beach

0. Write sentences about Coco Beach and Sandy Point Beach.

. _____

. _____

. _____

. _____

. _____

11. **Listen and repeat.**

I'd like to take a hike tomorrow.

He'd like to go to the beach tomorrow.

12. Say.

I'd like to go to the mountains on my vacation.

I'd like to visit a big city.

1. go / to the mountains on my vacation
2. take / a hike in the forest
3. visit / the zoo
4. take / photos of the river
5. eat / at the Star Café
6. buy / souvenirs in the shops

visit / a big city
go / to the beach
play / in the park
ride / in a boat on the lake
walk / to the hotel and rest
write / postcards to send

13. Look at 12. Write six things you'd like to do on vacation.

1. _____
2. _____
3. _____
4. _____
5. _____
6. _____

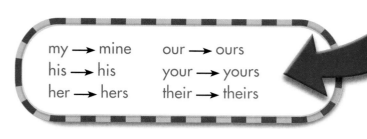

my → mine	our → ours
his → his	your → yours
her → hers	their → theirs

4. 🔘 **Listen and repeat.**

It's my letter. → It's mine.
It's your suitcase. → It's yours.
It's her camera. → It's hers.
It's his kite. → It's his.
It's our map. → It's ours.
They're your books. → They're yours.
They're their skateboards. → They're theirs.

5. Complete the chart.

Possessive Adjectives	Possessive Pronouns
It's my video game.	It's mine.
It's _____ pen.	It's yours.
They're her books.	They're _____
It's _____ cap.	It's his.
It's our motorcycle.	It's _____
They're your jackets.	They're _____
It's _____ kitten.	It's theirs.

6. Change the sentences.

1. That isn't Monique's camera. It's ~~Steve's camera.~~ *his*

2. That isn't Robert's plane ticket. It's Anne's.

3. That isn't David's backpack. It's your backpack.

4. These aren't your family's tickets. They're my family's tickets.

5. Those aren't Kevin's hiking boots. They're my hiking boots.

6. That isn't our map. It's Bill and Lola's map.

Vacation Days 29

Writing

17. Read.

Sentence Variety in a Paragraph

Use different kinds of sentences to make your paragraph interesting. Use some short sentences. Use some longer sentences with *and*, *but*, or *because*.

✕ **This paragraph isn't interesting because all the sentences are the same.**

> I had fun on my vacation. I went to the mountains. I went swimming. I went hiking. I walked around the town. I looked in all the shops. I bought some postcards. I bought some presents. I wanted to stay longer. I had fun. I had to come home. I'll go back next year.

✓ **This paragraph is more interesting because there are different kinds of sentences.**

> I had fun on my vacation in the mountains. I went swimming and hiking. I walked around the town, and I looked in all the shops. I bought some postcards and some presents. I wanted to stay longer because I had fun. I had to come home, but I'll go back next year.

18. Read Jane's paragraph.

My Day in the City

by Jane Davis

Yesterday was very exciting. I went to the city. I visited my aunt in a big apartment building. I rode in an elevator by myself. It was scary. I saw a lot of buildings in the city from her windows. I didn't see any trees. We ate lunch in a small café. We walked to a very big toy store. My aunt bought me a game. I didn't want to go home. We had a really good time. Next week, I'll visit my grandma in the country.

9. Make Jane's paragraph more interesting. Change some sentences. Use *and, but,* or *because.*

I went to the city. I visited my aunt in a big apartment building.

_____

I rode in an elevator by myself. It was scary.

_____

I saw a lot of buildings in the city from her windows. I didn't see any trees.

_____

We walked to a very big toy store. My aunt bought me a game.

_____

I didn't want to go home. We had a really good time.

_____

10. Write a paragraph about an exciting day.

_____

title

by _____

name

_____

_____

_____

_____

_____

Game Time

21.  **Play and say.**

His suitcase is as heavy as hers.

That's number one!

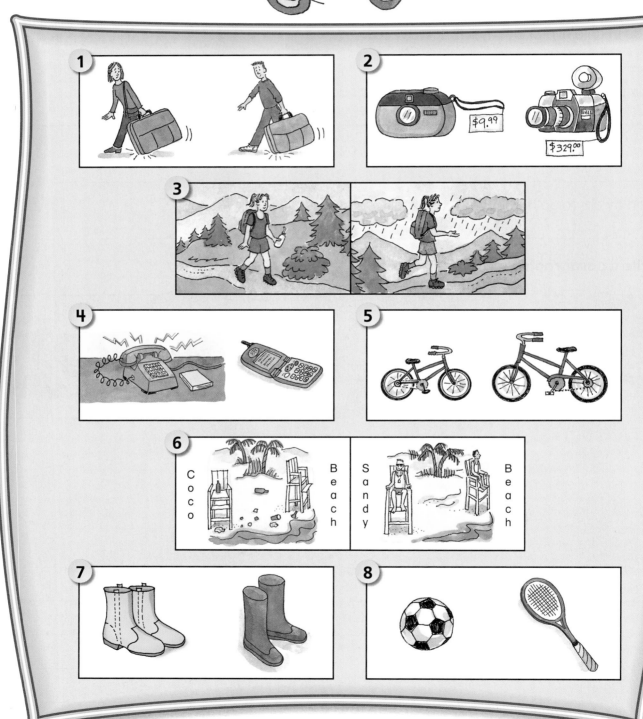

2. Read and discuss.

Think of Others

On vacation, share in activities that everyone wants to do.

Help Mom and Dad rest and relax.

3. Discuss the questions. Write.

. Why is it important to take turns doing activities on vacation?

_____

. How do you make vacations special for your mother and father?

_____

Let's Go Shopping

1. **Listen and repeat.**

① How much is that athletic equipment?

② Where is the computer store?

③ Do you like the striped blouse or the plain one?

④ Is she meeting us at the pet store?

⑤ Did you bring your credit card?

⑥ What are you going to buy?

⑦ Does Alice want a cat or a dog?

⑧ Are you tired of shopping?

2. **Describe the picture.**

3. **Listen and repeat. Role-play.**

① I don't know. What do you think?

② It looks good, but it's very expensive.

③ Maybe I should try on the brown jacket again.

④ It doesn't look as good as that one, but it's cheaper.

4. **Listen. Sing or chant.**

Song

Shopping

Do you sell shoes and winter boots?
Do you have winter jackets?
I'm looking for some story books.
Where are the tennis racquets?

How much is that camera?
How much is that ball?
I'm looking for a video game.
Will I find it at the mall?

Which stores sell toys and food for cats?
Is the jewelry store nearby?
I'm looking for a pretty ring.
Please, help me find a tie.

Do you like shopping at the mall?
What do you like the best?
I'm looking for a place to sit.
I need a place to rest!

Is the store open? Yes, it is.
Did you go to the mall? No, I didn't.

5. A28 **Listen and repeat.**

Is the chair expensive?
Was he comfortable in the chair?
Are they going to buy the chair?

Did Mae buy new sneakers?
Do you like to go to the mall?
Does he shop on weekends?

6. Change the sentences into questions.

1. Jim is going to buy a new video game.

Is Jim going to buy a new video game?

2. The yellow bike is the most expensive.

_____

3. Julio was excited about his new skateboard.

_____

4. Alicia and Carmen want new tennis racquets.

_____

5. Laura bought a present for her mother.

_____

7. Write questions for the answers.

1. _____

Yes, he wants the plaid shirt.

2. _____

Yes, they are at the mall.

3. _____

No, they didn't go shopping.

4. _____

No, Sally wasn't in school yesterday.

what
when
where
how much

A29

8. **Listen and repeat.**

What did she buy?

When are we going to eat lunch?

Where did you get your sunglasses?

How much did he pay for that camera?

A30

9. **Listen to the questions about Angela. Circle the best answers.**

food court

clothing store

sports equipment store

1. (She's at the food court.)   She's eating some pizza.

2. She went to the clothing store.   She bought a skirt.

3. They're going to eat lunch at noon.   They're going to eat lunch at the deli.

4. She paid ten dollars for the ball.   She bought four balls.

5. She went to the clothing store after she ate lunch.   She paid $14.00 for that shirt.

6. She went to the sports equipment store.   She bought a hockey stick.

7. The burger cost five dollars.   She got the burger at the Burger Den.

8. They like shopping at the mall.   They're going to the clothing store.

Go to Cool Clothes.
Don't go to Cathy's Clothes.

10. A37 **Listen and repeat.**

Look at these shoes!
Try on that jacket.

Don't buy that computer.
Please don't shop anymore!

11. Complete the sentences.

try on

put back

1. (sit)   Louisa, _____ *sit* _____ down and rest a minute.

2. (put back)   _____ that video game. No more toys!

3. (try on/neg.)   _____ the blue dress. The red one is prettier.

4. (call)   _____ me when you get home from the mall.

5. (do)   _____ your homework before you go out.

6. (touch/neg.)   _____ any toys on the shelf.

7. (buy)   _____ that for your sister. She'll love it!

12. A32 **Listen and write.**

| get | look | meet | put on | take |

Mom, (1) _____ at this ad in the paper!

(2) _____ me to the SuperMall. Please?

OK. (3) _____ your money!

(4)_____ your coat and

(5)_____ me at the car.

This coat is too small.
It isn't big enough.

13. **Listen and repeat.**

That camera is too expensive.
I only have $25.00 to buy a present.

Those boots aren't big enough.
I need a bigger size.

$329.⁰⁰

14. Match the sentences with similar meanings.

1. This blouse isn't big enough.　　　　　a. I bought more than I need.

2. This shirt is too small.　　　　　　　b. It's too small.

3. That jacket is too expensive.　　　　　c. It's too short.

4. These dresses are too plain.　　　　　d. It isn't big enough.

5. I bought too many things.　　　　　　e. They aren't dressy enough.

6. Those bikes aren't new.　　　　　　　f. They aren't big enough.

7. That skirt isn't long enough.　　　　　g. It isn't cheap enough.

8. These sneakers are too small.　　　　　h. They're too old.

15. Write two sentences for each picture.

short / long

big / small

plain / dressy

expensive / cheap

1. The shirt sleeves are too short. They aren't long enough.

2. _____

3. _____

4. _____

Writing

16. Read.

Unity in a Paragraph

All the sentences in a paragraph should talk about the main idea of the paragraph. After you write a paragraph, look for sentences that don't belong and take them out.

I like to shop for old books. I like to go to the bookstores that sell books that are more than 100 years old. ~~My father loves books about sports.~~ Old books tell a lot about how people lived and dressed and what they did every day. I like to learn about children who were my age long ago. ~~My mother reads a lot.~~ Some old books are written on very thin paper. Sometimes the print is very small. ~~My mother wears glasses to read.~~ I could shop for old books every day.

17. Read Luke's paragraph. Which sentences don't belong? Cross them out.

Sunday Shopping

by Luke Williams

I shop with my father on Sunday, but we don't go shopping at the mall. We shop at an outdoor market where people sell stamps. My father and I collect stamps from different countries. My sister has eleven Barbie dolls. We like to look for stamps with nice drawings and colors. We have beautiful stamps from Guatemala, Venezuela, Costa Rica, Canada, Russia, Korea, Taiwan, and Japan. E-mails don't need stamps. This Sunday we are going to look for a special stamp from Egypt. If the stamp is too expensive, my father will help me pay for it. I like to play video games, too.

18. Read the sentences. Complete the paragraph below with six of the sentences.

1. First, I buy notebooks of different colors for my classes.
2. Math class is the hardest for me.
3. Then I choose pencils, pens, and markers of many colors.
4. I usually buy a special pencil case to hold all my pencils and pens.
5. I like to write with pens more than with pencils.
6. After I choose a pencil case, I get tape and glue.
7. My old backpack is yellow and black.
8. Finally, I get a ruler and a calculator.
9. I like to buy new supplies for school every year.

Shopping for School Supplies

I love to shop for school supplies. _____

_____

_____

_____

_____

_____

_____

_____

_____

_____

_____

19. Look at the paragraphs you wrote for Units 1, 2, and 3 (on pages 9, 19, and 31).
Are there any sentences that do not belong? Cross them out.

Game Time

20. Play and say. Work with a partner. Take turns. Close your eyes and point to a box. Make a question to match the answer in your box. Then it's your partner's turn.

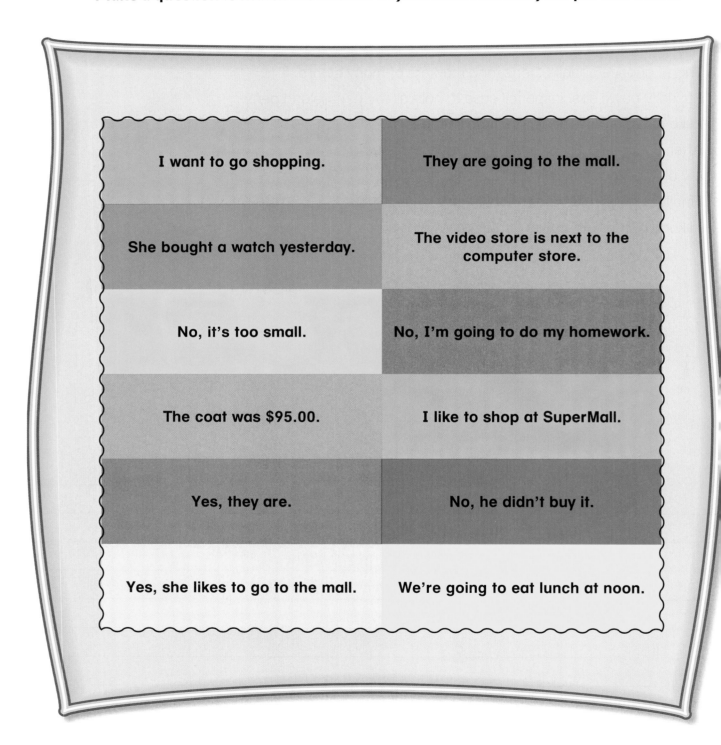

I want to go shopping.	They are going to the mall.
She bought a watch yesterday.	The video store is next to the computer store.
No, it's too small.	No, I'm going to do my homework.
The coat was $95.00.	I like to shop at SuperMall.
Yes, they are.	No, he didn't buy it.
Yes, she likes to go to the mall.	We're going to eat lunch at noon.

21. Read and discuss.

Giving Is Important

Having more things does not mean having more happiness.

Sharing what you already have brings happiness.

22. Discuss the questions. Write.

1. How can having too many clothes, toys, and other things be bad?

_____

2. How can you share things you have that you don't need anymore?

_____

Shopping Here and There

Where do you like to go shopping? Outdoor markets? Department stores? What about online stores? If you like to shop, there are lots of ways you can buy what you need. Let's imagine you want to buy some new clothes.

Some people go to outdoor markets to buy and sell clothing and other goods. It's fun to browse the clothing stands at outdoor markets. Shoppers like to walk around and see all the unique products. These markets are usually open one day a week or once a month.

At some outdoor markets, the sellers and buyers haggle over the price. *Haggle* means the seller and buyer discuss and sometimes decide the price between themselves. This makes it difficult to compare prices at an outdoor market. Buyers have to walk around and ask each seller how much the product costs.

If you don't want to buy your clothes at an outdoor market, you can go to a department store. Some people like to shop in big department stores. Buyers can see the price on a price tag, so it's easier to compare two brands. Shoppers also like department stores because they can try on the clothes in the fitting room. Best of all, sometimes there's a sale, and some brands cost less money. Look for "Sale" signs by the clothing you like.

Other shoppers use the Internet for online shopping. Department stores in many towns and cities offer catalogs online. You can shop, order, and pay with a credit card . . . all online. Imagine, you can shop in your pajamas and buy your new clothes without leaving your house!

So, how do you like to shop?

UNIT 5

What Happened?

1. **Listen and repeat.**

1. Last Saturday morning, the sun was shining brightly.

2. The birds were singing loudly.

3. The wind was blowing softly while we rode down the river in our boat.

4. By 10:00, dark gray clouds were moving swiftly across the sky. Then it started to rain.

5. Our boat wasn't moving quickly enough. We were getting wet!

6. It was impossible to keep the boat steady while it was raining.

7. The water was flowing very fast.

8. Rain was filling our boat while we rowed. Finally we saw the boathouse!

2. **Describe the pictures.**

Listen and repeat. Role-play.

① Oh, no! What happened?

② I was riding my bike when I saw my friend's cat in a tree.

③ Was your friend looking for it?

④ Yes. But he couldn't get the cat, so I climbed the tree.

⑤ Then what happened?

⑥ The cat jumped on me, and I fell out of the tree onto my bike!

Listen. Sing or chant.

 Song

An Adventure in the Park

I was walking around
  in the park one night.
And then what happened?
What happened?

I heard something moving,
  which gave me a fright!
And then what happened?
What happened?

A bear was staring me
  right in the face!
And then what happened?
What happened?

I quickly turned 'round
  and froze in my place.
And then what happened?
I screamed! *Aaaahhhhh!*

I was reading last night.
We were talking on the phone.

5. Listen and repeat.

The sun was shining all day.

They were skateboarding until dark.

6. Write.

snow

wait in line

turn on

1. (snow) Sue looked out the window. It _____was snowing_____ !

2. (wait) *Andy's Adventure* was a very popular movie. People _____
in line for a long time.

3. (come) Carlos turned on his flashlight. A bear _____ toward his tent!

4. (rain) It _____ all day yesterday.

5. (blow) The wind _____ for hours.

6. (make) The children _____ a lot of noise inside.

7. Write about yourself.

1. What were you doing last night at 9:00?

_____

2. What were you doing yesterday morning at 10:00?

_____

While I was washing the car, it began to rain.

A39 **Listen and repeat.**

While they were playing a game, the phone rang.

The phone rang while they were playing a game.

Unscramble and write. Then choose and match.

. snack / be / a / make / while / I

<u>While I was making a snack,</u>

a. the lights went out.

. play / he / while / be / piano / the

_____

b. my sister drank my juice.

. be / she / a / read / book / while

_____

c. he fell out of the chair.

. we / bikes / our / ride / be / while

_____

d. they ran out of film.

. shower / he / a / take / be / while

_____

e. it began to rain.

. be / an / eat / apple / while / I

_____

f. the telephone rang.

. photos / they / take / while / be

_____

g. I saw my friend Jack.

. while / tree / a / be / I / climb

_____

h. a tooth came out.

0. Look at 9. Work with a partner. Say.

What happened?

My sister drank my juice while I was making a snack.

What Happened?

11. Listen and repeat.

Rosa studies hard.
She does her homework carefully.
She reads quietly.
She works patiently.

12. Complete the sentences.

1. (quiet)   Carlos turned on his flashlight _____ quietly _____.

2. (quick)   She ran _____ when it started to rain.

3. (loud)   The dog barked _____ when the doorbell rang.

4. (soft)   The rain fell _____ all afternoon.

5. (hard)   Study _____ and you will do well.

6. (careful)   She makes her jewelry _____.

7. (patient)   They waited in line _____ for movie tickets.

13. Write sentences.

turtle

library

row

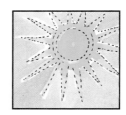

shine

brightly   fast   loudly   slowly

1. _____

2. _____

3. _____

4. _____

4. Listen and repeat.

> Your dog runs more quickly than mine.

Marta sings loudly.
Carmen sings more loudly than Marta.
Lucia sings as loudly as Carmen.
Gloria sings the most loudly of all the singers.

5. Listen and take notes. Then write sentences.

	Ella	Ashley	Jessica
1. runs (fast)	as fast as Ashley	fast	
2. talks (softly)	the most softly	more softly than Jessica	softly
3. draws (quickly)			
4. speaks (clearly)			
5. studies (quietly)			
6. eats (slowly)			

1. Ella runs _as fast as Ashley_____.

2. Jessica talks _____.

3. Ella draws _____.

4. Ashley speaks _____.

5. Ella studies _____.

6. Jessica eats _____.

6. Talk about your family.

I climb trees more quickly than my brother does.

My mother eats the most slowly of all.

Writing

17. Read.

Informal Letters

Letters to family and friends are called informal letters. An informal letter has five parts:

| heading | greeting | body | closing | signature |

18. Read Yoko's letter to her friend. Notice the five parts.

heading — *Greenleaf Park
Sunday, August 12*

Dear Barbara, — greeting

body —
I want to tell you about my camping trip at Greenleaf Park. The first two days were wonderful. The sun was shining brightly in the blue sky while we fished, hiked, and swam in the lake. On the third day, the sky got gray and cloudy, and the wind blew very fast. I was quietly taking photos of some beautiful birds when it began to rain really hard. The sky got very dark, and the rain was falling harder and faster. I was running when lightning hit a tree in front of me! My friends were looking for me when I got back to camp. It was the scariest experience of my life!

Love, — closing

Yoko — signature

me

9. **Choose one of the pictures and describe what happened in an informal letter to a friend. Include the five parts from 17.**

20. **Work with a partner. Read your partner's letter. Does it describe an adventure based on one of the pictures? Is the letter clear? Does it have the five parts?**

Game Time

21. 💬 **Play and say.**

Number one.

1 and D. While she was hiking, it began to rain.

1-5 ➡️
1. hike
2. take / a shower
3. walk / home
4. lie / on the beach
5. open / the door

a. telephone / ring
b. dog / bark
c. see / a fire truck
d. begin / to rain
e. wind / begin to blow
⬅️ **A-E**

Finished? Now make different sentences of your own.

2. Read and discuss.

Be Prepared

Safety first.
Always have an adventure buddy and the equipment you need with you.

3. Discuss the questions. Write.

Why is it important to have at least one other person with you?

_____

What do you need in a first-aid kit? Why?

_____

Communicating

B1

1. **Listen and repeat.**

① Will you help me get on the Internet?

② Sure.

③ Will you fix my computer, please?

④ Sorry. I won't have time today.

⑤ Will you send this fax for me, please?

⑥ OK. Put it on my desk.

COPIER IS BROKEN

LIBRARY

Everyone is very busy.
Someone is sending a fax.
Someone is reading a magazine.
Someone is using the printer.
Someone is studying the globe.
Someone is having trouble with a computer.
No one is making copies.
No one is answering the telephone.

2. **Describe the picture.**

Listen and repeat. Role-play.

① What's the matter?

② I don't know. Someone used my cell phone, and now it doesn't work right.

③ Is your battery good?

④ Yes. Will you take a look at it, please?

⑤ Sure. No problem.

⑥ I really appreciate it. Thanks.

Listen. Sing or chant.

 Song

Communicating 24/7

Will you please call me later?
I'll call you on my cell phone.
Will you please send me your address?
I'll send it when I get home.

Call me. Send me a fax.
I'll try to keep in touch.
Write me a letter every day!
Isn't that too much?

I will send you an e-mail.
You have that much to say?
Will you please send me an answer?
I won't. I'm busy today.

Call me. Send me a card.
Maybe I'll keep in touch.
Oh, come on. Just a letter.
You communicate too much!

5.  **Listen and repeat.**

Everyone is wearing a red shirt.   Someone is wearing a red shirt.   No one is wearing a red shirt.

6. Write *everyone*, *no one*, or *someone*.

1. _____ knows the price of the video camera.

2. Will _____ please send this fax for me?

3. _____ in the park is talking on a cell phone!

7. Complete the sentences. Use *everyone*, *someone*, or *no one*.

1. _____ is playing a board game.

_____ is reading a book.

2. Look! There's _____ in the candy store!

3. _____ is riding a bike.

_____ is wearing a yellow shirt.

8. Write a sentence about your class. Use *everyone*, *someone*, or *no one*.

_____

Will you help me, please?

Will you help me fix the copy machine? OK.
Will you turn off your cell phone, please? Sure I will.
Will you move her computer today? Sorry. I'm too busy.

10. Write. Then ask and answer.

fix   give   help   mail   ~~meet~~   move

1. ___Will___ you ___meet___ me in front of the video store, please?

2. _____ you _____ this letter for me, please?

3. _____ you _____ him with his homework, please?

4. _____ you _____ this book to your sister, please?

5. _____ you _____ your coat, please? It's on my chair.

6. _____ you _____ his computer, please?

11. Look and write questions.

Sure. I'll call Keiko later.

1   call

No, I won't clean my room!

2   clean

Yes, I'll make a copy for you.

3   make a copy

1. _____

2. _____

3. _____

Who **did** you call?
I **called** my mother.

12. B6 **Listen and repeat.**

Who does she visit every weekend?
She visits her cousin.

Who is Andy calling?
He's calling David.

13. Write questions.

1. _Who do you want to invite to our computer club meeting?_

I want to invite **Kenji** to our computer club meeting.

2. _____

I wrote to my **grandmother**.

3. _____

I visited **my uncle and aunt** on Saturday.

4. _____

Li-Ping usually e-mails **his friend in Mexico**.

5. _____

Maria always plays with **her friends** on the weekend.

6. _____

I'm going to invite **everyone in our class** to my party.

14. Ask and answer with a partner.

walk / to school / with

Mark

play / chess / with

Sonia

go / to the movies / with

my sister

watch / TV / with

my friend Joe

 Unit 6

Who called you?
My mom called me.

15. **Listen and repeat.**

Who is listening to that radio?
　　Carmen is listening to that radio.

Who has my magazines?
　　Donna has your magazines.

16. Ask and answer with a partner. Then write.

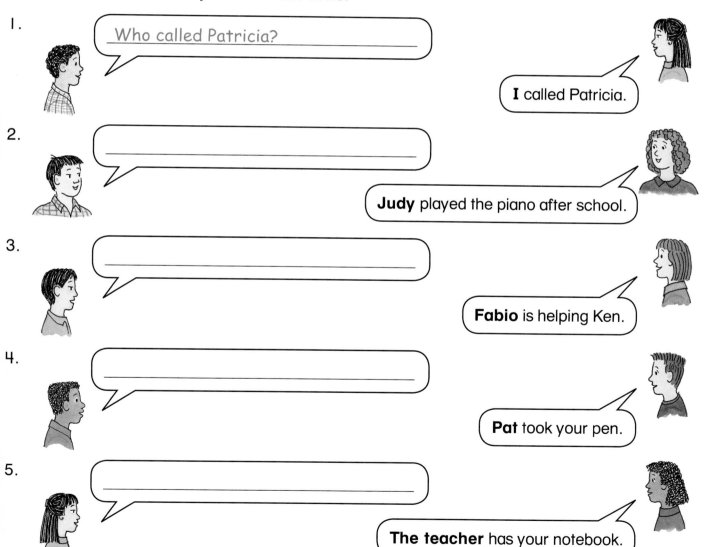

1. Who called Patricia?

I called Patricia.

2. _____

Judy played the piano after school.

3. _____

Fabio is helping Ken.

4. _____

Pat took your pen.

5. _____

The teacher has your notebook.

Writing

17. Read.

Formal Letters

When we write to a business or to a person we don't know, we use the formal letter style. A formal letter has five parts:

> heading   greeting   body   closing   signature

18. Read the ad and Steve's formal letter. Label the parts.

Video Games
new and used

We have exciting new video games
at the best prices.
You'll be amazed at our large collection.
Request our latest catalog.

Write: Mr. Frank Silva
347 Dover Street
Westport, New York 10139

164 Kingston Street
Centerville, Michigan 49148
October 17, 2 _ _ _

Mr. Frank Silva
347 Dover Street
Westport, New York 10139

Dear Mr. Silva:

I saw your ad in the newspaper today. I am 12 years old, and I like to play video games. I know a lot about them. Will you please send me your newest catalog? Thank you.

Sincerely,

Steve Wilson

Steve Wilson

19. Read the ads. Write a formal letter asking about a cell phone or an electronics catalog.

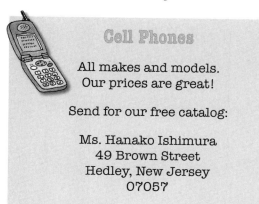

Cell Phones

All makes and models.
Our prices are great!

Send for our free catalog:

Ms. Hanako Ishimura
49 Brown Street
Hedley, New Jersey
07057

We buy and sell the latest electronics!

Free catalog
Contact: Mr. George Grant
1806 Sixth Avenue
Ellsworth, California
94119

20. Work with a partner. Read your partner's letter. Is the letter clear? Does it have the five parts?

Game Time

21. **Play and say.**
    Make two questions for each answer. Each correct question is one point!

 Who did Maria visit?

 What did Maria do last night?

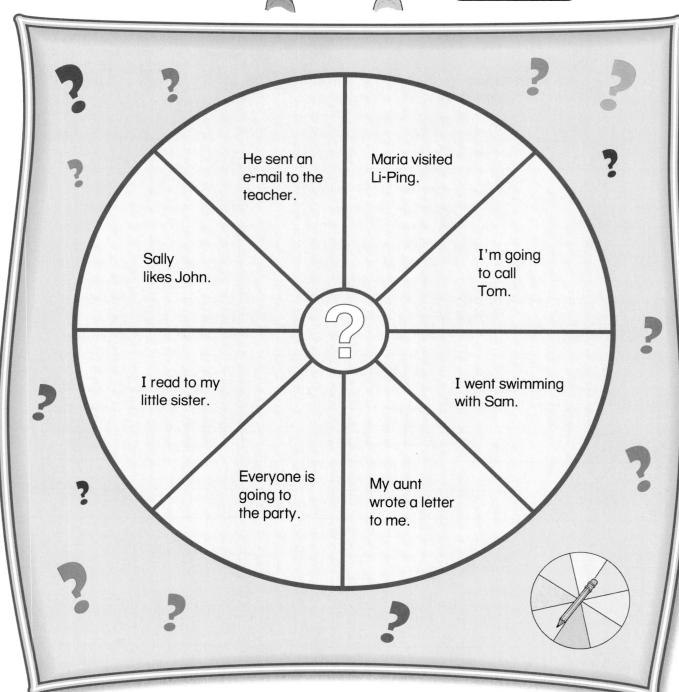

He sent an e-mail to the teacher.

Maria visited Li-Ping.

Sally likes John.

I'm going to call Tom.

I read to my little sister.

I went swimming with Sam.

Everyone is going to the party.

My aunt wrote a letter to me.

22. **Read and discuss.**

Be Helpful

Help your neighbors.

Help people at school.

23. **Discuss the questions. Write.**

1. Do you notice when people need help?

_____

2. What do you do to help people?

_____

READING B8 The Great White Storm

A storm with very fast winds and very heavy snow is called a *blizzard*. Its winds can be greater than 45 miles (72 km) per hour. (That's as fast as a car!) Visibility falls to under a quarter of a mile (402 m). Blizzards usually happen during the winter months (December, January, and February in the United States), and so the blizzard of 1888 was a big surprise.

On March 12, 1888, the temperature dropped below freezing and the wind blew faster than usual, reaching blizzard conditions. Snow started to fall and continued falling and falling. This blizzard soon became one of the most famous snowstorms in United States history. It was called "The Great White Storm." There were worse blizzards before 1888, and there have been worse blizzards since then. But the blizzard of 1888, especially its effect on New York City, captures the American imagination.

The days before the blizzard were warm, but then the wind started blowing and the temperature dropped. By the end of the storm, 40 inches (1 m) of snow covered city streets. Transportation became impossible, and people were trapped in their homes and on the trains. Telephone and telegraph wires snapped, so no one could communicate. The wind blew ships up onto shore, and fire trucks were buried in giant snow drifts. More than 400 people died. Everyone had a story to tell about the adventure.

One good thing did come out of "The Great White Storm." Many people in New York City were riding elevated trains when it began to snow. Riders became trapped in cold cars when the trains stalled from the storm, so people began to think of ways to prepare for the next big storm. One idea was to build an underground railroad. A few years later, New York City approved plans for its first subway.

Inventions

1. B9 **Listen and repeat.**

What do you think it is?

It might be a pen.

Oh, it's a flashlight.

It may be a clock.

Oh, it's a compass.

Oh, it's a telescope.

It might be a camera.

It may be a skateboard.

Oh, it's a scooter.

2. **Describe the pictures.**

① What's that?

② I don't know. I found it in the street.

③ It might be an MP3 player.

④ No, I don't think so.

⑤ Maybe it's a special kind of car key.

⑥ It may be a calculator. Who knows?

B11 **Listen. Sing or chant.**

Song

What in the World Is That?

Hey, look! Look up there!
Do you see that thing?
Do you see that thing?
What in the world is that?

I'm not sure. I really don't know.
It might be a star.
It may be a plane.
It might be a UFO!

Hey, look! Look down there!
Do you see that thing?
Do you see that thing?
What in the world is that?

I'm not sure. I really don't know.
It might be a shark.
It may be a ray.
I don't care—let's go!

I may go to the movies.
It might rain tomorrow.

5. **Listen and repeat.**

It's hot today.
I might go to the beach.

Someone's at the door.
It may be my friend Julia.

6. Write sentences. Use *may* or *might*.

1   2   3   4   5   6   7

1. (go / this afternoon) _I may go skateboarding this afternoon._

2. (use / later) _____

3. (do / after dinner) _____

4. (go / on Saturday) _____

5. (ride / tomorrow) _____

6. (take / at the soccer game) _____

7. (make / for dessert) _____

7. **What are you going to do this weekend? Tell a partner. Use *may* and *might*.**

I might go shopping on Saturday.
What about you?

I'm not sure. I may go to the park, or
I may go to the movies.

8. Read. Then unscramble and write.

The Case of the Missing Invention
Jack made an invention for the school's science fair. It's time to show his invention to the judges, but his invention isn't there!

Where is Jack's invention?

1. may / table / under / be / it / the

  It may be under the table.

table

2. closet / may / in / it / be / the

_____

closet

3. hallway / be / the / it / in / may

_____

hallway

4. on / it / staircase / might / the / be

_____

staircase

5. be / might / the / garbage / it / in

_____

garbage

6. Jane's / might / in / desk / be / it

_____

desk

Inventions 71

Use a spoon to eat your soup.

9.  **Listen and repeat.**

They went to the store to buy a new cell phone.
I turned off the TV to study better.

You may listen to the radio to find out the weather.
You might use a knife to cut a cake.

10. **Work with a partner. Ask and answer.**

1. Why did you turn on the TV?

2. Why did you call your friend?

3. Why do you go to school?

4. Why did you sleep late?

5. Why do you do homework?

6. Why do you listen to the radio?

11. How might you use these objects? Write.

| hold down papers | hold toys | hold up books | make a necklace |
| make a paper airplane | make a paper hat | play a game | ~~stand on~~ |

a pot

a brick

paper clips

a newspaper

You might use a pot

to stand on
_____

_____

You may use a brick

_____

_____

You may use paper clips

_____

_____

You might use a newspaper

_____

_____

do → did → done

study → studied → studied

12. **Listen and repeat.**

I write letters to Jordi all the time.
I wrote him a letter last week.
Jordi has written me eight times.

13. Use the verbs in the chart to make sentences. Use the pictures for ideas.

Regular Verb Base Form	Simple Past	Past Participle
call	called	called
dance	danced	danced
receive	received	received
study	studied	studied
talk	talked	talked
use	used	used

Irregular Verb Base Form	Simple Past	Past Participle
begin	began	begun
bring	brought	brought
cut	cut	cut
do	did	done
go	went	gone
grow	grew	grown
make	made	made
put	put	put
run	ran	run
sell	sold	sold
sing	sang	sung
swim	swam	swum
take	took	taken
write	wrote	written

Writing

14. Read.

Describing an Object

Use details when you write about an object, such as an invention or a favorite thing. Specific details make your writing interesting. Include information about your object's size, color, shape, use, and other characteristics. This helps your reader "see" the object.

Size	Color	Shape	Use
large	blue	rectangular	to cut with
long	bright	round	to drink from
thick	colorful	square	to keep things in
tiny	pale	triangular	to write with

15. Read Hee Jung's paragraph about an object. Notice how she describes size, color, shape, and use.

A Wonderful Walking Stick

by Hee Jung Choi

One of my favorite objects is my uncle Min Ho's walking stick. It is very special to me. The stick part is long and thin. It is made of dark, shiny wood the color of chocolate. At the top of the stick part is a ring made of silver. On top of the ring is a round ball made of glass. It is a beautiful dark blue, and you can see some bubbles inside the glass. Someone painted the blue glass ball to look like a map of the world. All the countries are painted different shades of green. When you use this wonderful stick to walk with, you have the world in your hand.

6. Choose an object to describe. List its details in the chart.

Size	
Color	
Shape	
Use	
(Other)	

7. Describe your object. Use Hee Jung's paragraph as a model.

_____
title

by _____

_____

_____

_____

_____

_____

_____

_____

8. Work with a partner. Read your partner's paragraph. What descriptive details can you find?

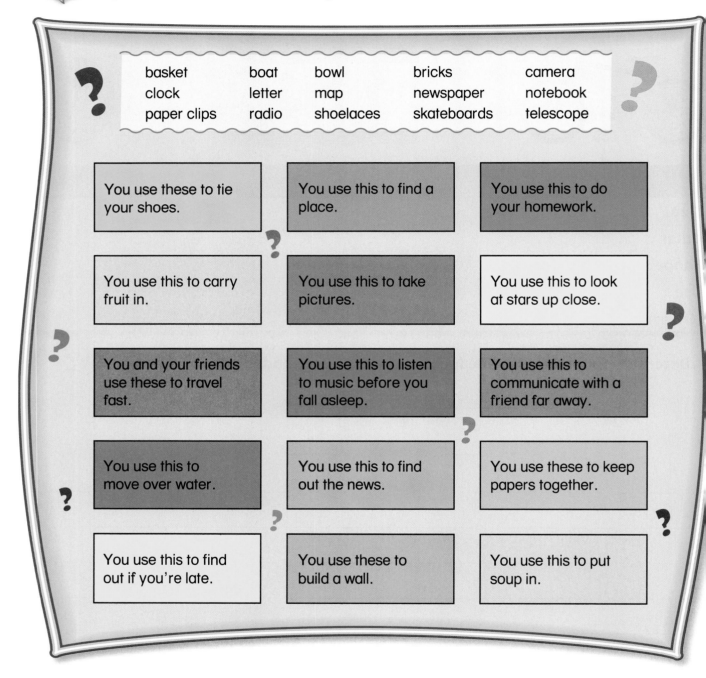

Game Time

19. **Play and say.** Take turns matching.

basket	boat	bowl	bricks	camera
clock	letter	map	newspaper	notebook
paper clips	radio	shoelaces	skateboards	telescope

You use these to tie your shoes.

You use this to find a place.

You use this to do your homework.

You use this to carry fruit in.

You use this to take pictures.

You use this to look at stars up close.

You and your friends use these to travel fast.

You use this to listen to music before you fall asleep.

You use this to communicate with a friend far away.

You use this to move over water.

You use this to find out the news.

You use these to keep papers together.

You use this to find out if you're late.

You use these to build a wall.

You use this to put soup in.

20. **Now make up new sentences and play again.**

You might use these to hold your hair back.

They're shoelaces! My turn.

21. 💬 **Read and discuss.**

Be Creative

2. 💬 **Discuss the questions. Write.**

. How are the children in the pictures creative?

_____

. Describe something creative you or a family member did.

_____

From Process to Product

B15

1. Listen and repeat.

How Pencils Are Made

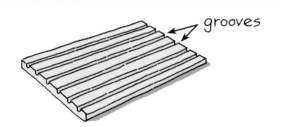

grooves

1. Grooves are cut into a piece of wood.

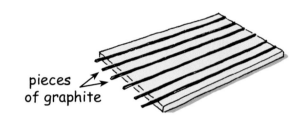

pieces of graphite

2. Long pieces of graphite are put into the grooves.

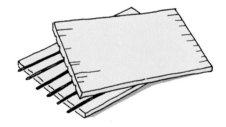

3. More wood is placed over the grooves.

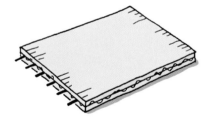

4. The two pieces of wood are glued together.

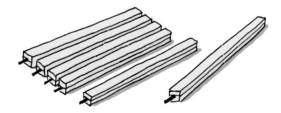

5. The wood is separated into strips.

6. The strips are shaped and painted.

2. Describe the pictures.

Listen and repeat. Role-play.

① What's next?

② It says, "Part D is placed inside Part B."

③ But I put Part C into Part B.

④ I don't think that's right.

⑤ Well, Part C is screwed into the bottom of Part B. Now I can't get it out.

⑥ Give me the screwdriver. Maybe I can separate them.

 **Listen. Sing or chant.**

B17

Song

My Thingamajig*

Could you help me out here?
Please—lend me a hand.
Go and find my thingamajig,
    the one with the metal band.

You'll know it when you see it.
It's made of strips of wood.
Please, help me find my thingamajig.
I'd be so happy if you would.

You'll see it in the closet
    or somewhere on the floor.
I think I left my thingamajig
    somewhere near the door.

Meanwhile I'll keep looking,
    but time is passing fast.
What is that you're saying?
My thingamajig is found at last!

Thingamajig is a word you can use when you don't know or don't remember the name of something.

This wall is made of brick.

5. **Listen and repeat.**

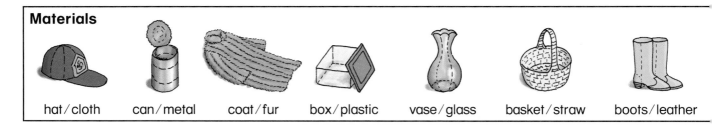

The fish tank is made of glass.   The baskets are made of straw.   The ball is made of plastic.

6. What is it made of? What are they made of? Ask and answer.

Materials

hat / cloth   can / metal   coat / fur   box / plastic   vase / glass   basket / straw   boots / leather

7. What is it made of? What are they made of? Write.

1.   The baskets are made of straw. _____

straw baskets

2. _____

a fur hat

3. _____

paper birds

4. _____

a leather jacket

5. _____

metal pens

6. _____

a plastic bottle

The pencils are painted.

8. Listen and repeat.

How are pencils made? Here are some steps.

Grooves are cut into a piece of wood.
Graphite is put into the grooves.
More wood is glued on top of the graphite.
The wood is separated into strips.
The strips are shaped and painted.

9. Look at the pictures and at the verb chart. Then write.

Base Form ⟶	Participle	Base Form ⟶	Participle
add	added	pour	poured
enjoy	enjoyed	put	put
fill	filled	stir	stirred

1. (put)   Tea leaves _____ into a teapot.

2. (fill)   The teapot _____ with very hot water.

3. (pour)   The tea _____ into cups.

4. (add)   Sometimes sugar and milk _____.

5. (stir)   The tea, sugar, and milk _____ together.

6. (enjoy)   The tea _____ by everyone.

10. How are flowers grown? Look at the pictures and at the verb chart. Take turns saying the sentences. Then write.

Base Form →	Participle	Base Form →	Participle
dig	dug	place	placed
move	moved	put	put
open	opened	water	watered

1. dirt / put / into a pot

  Dirt is put into a pot.

2. a hole / dig / in the dirt

_____

3. a package of seeds / open

_____

4. seeds / place / in the hole

_____

5. the seeds / water

_____

6. the pot / move / to a sunny place

_____

Learn and Practice

The Costa Rican rain forest is beautiful.

11. B20 **Listen and repeat.**

a camera from Germany → a German camera
tea from China → Chinese tea
chocolate from Mexico → Mexican chocolate
cell phones from Japan → Japanese cell phones
rings from Venezuela → Venezuelan rings

12. B21 **Listen and repeat. Write the numbers. Then write sentences.**

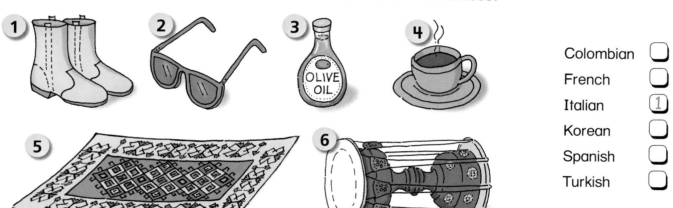

Colombian	☐
French	☐
Italian	1
Korean	☐
Spanish	☐
Turkish	☐

1. I like this coffee from Colombia.
   I like this Colombian coffee.

2. Look at the colors in that rug from Turkey.
   _____

3. This olive oil from Spain is delicious.
   _____

4. He wants some boots from Italy.
   _____

5. My brother has a drum from Korea.
   _____

6. She bought some sunglasses from France.
   _____

13. Read.

> **Describing a Process: Sequence Words**
>
> **Use sequence words when you describe the steps in a process or procedure.**
>
> ### How Tea Is Made
>
> First, tea leaves are put into a teapot.
> Second, the teapot is filled with very hot water.
> Third, the tea is poured into cups.
> Next, sugar and milk are added to taste.
> Then, the tea is stirred with a spoon.
> Finally, the tea is enjoyed by everyone.

14. Read Laura's paragraph. Underline the sequence words.

How Fruit Salad Is Made

by Laura Rivas

This is how my favorite fruit salad is made: First, yogurt is put into a bowl. Second, a mango and a banana are cut up into pieces. Third, some strawberries are cut up. Next, the fruit is added to the bowl with the yogurt. Then, sugar is stirred into the yogurt and fruit. Finally, my fruit salad is served in a pretty bowl. It's delicious!

5. Look and read. Number the steps in sequence.

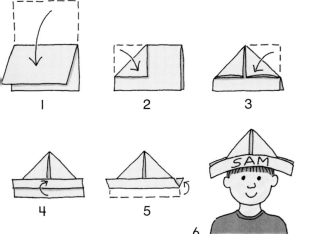

1

2

3

4

5

6

How a Paper Hat Is Made

___ The top left corner is folded down.

___ The front side of the bottom is folded up.

___ The top right corner is folded down.

___ Your hat is placed on your head.

___ The other side of the bottom is folded up.

_1_ A piece of paper is folded in half.

6. Work with a partner. Look at 15. Describe how a paper hat is made.

7. Describe how hot chocolate is made. Use Laura's paragraph as a model.

_____
title

by _____
name

_____

_____

_____

_____

_____

_____

_____

18. Write each base form and its participle in any circle.

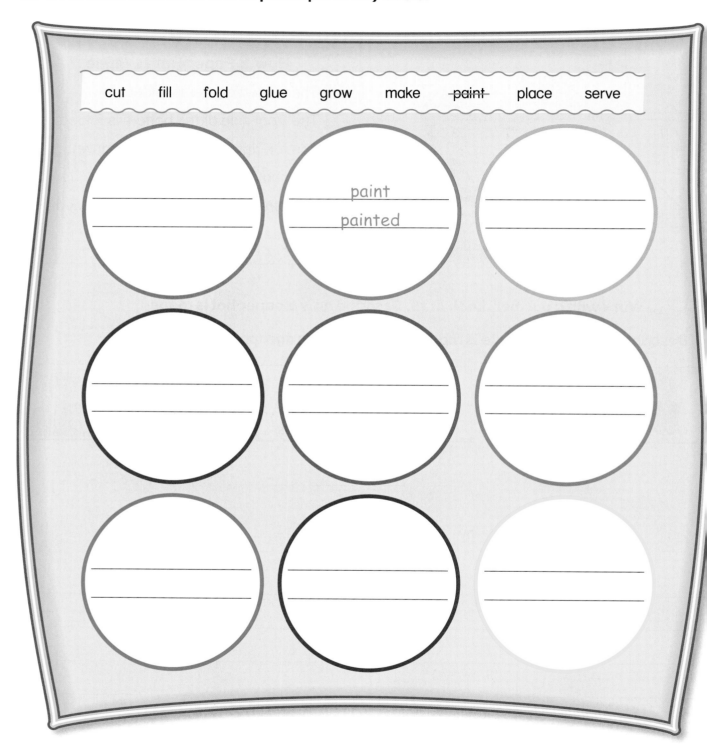

cut   fill   fold   glue   grow   make   ~~paint~~   place   serve

paint
painted

19. Listen to the sentences. When you hear a participle, write a big X in the circle. When you get three circles in a row, say "Bingo!"

20. Read and discuss.

Work Carefully

Follow all instructions.

Don't hurry to finish quickly. Check your work.

1. Discuss the questions. Write.

. Do you like to work slowly or quickly? Why?

_____

. Describe a time you didn't work carefully. What happened?

_____

READING B23 — Speaking Without Sound

Everyone has to communicate. For deaf people, it's difficult to use only spoken language. Special languages called *sign languages* were invented as a way to communicate without speaking. In sign languages, most signs are made by hand movements, but facial expressions and body movements are important, too.

Many families with deaf members make up their own signs, but using a standardized sign language really opens the doors for communication. One standardized sign language, American Sign Language (ASL), was

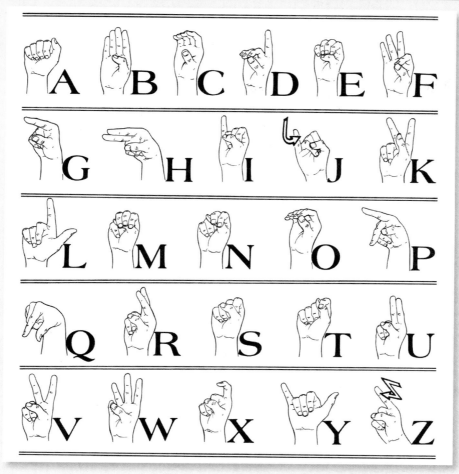

Drawing of the ASL manual alphabet

created in the United States in 1817 at a school for the deaf in Hartford, Connecticut. Graduates of this school taught ASL in schools for the deaf all over the country. Now ASL is used across the United States.

ASL is a unique language with its own rules. It is different from sign languages used in other countries. Users of Spanish Sign Language or British Sign Language, for example, can understand very little of American Sign Language.

Like any other language, ASL is always growing and changing. Signers make new signs to keep up with changes in the modern world. ASL users can communicate very complex ideas and emotions. They see their language as a valuable part of their culture.

Let's Do Something

1. B24 **Listen and repeat.**

① Let's watch a game show.

② I'd rather watch the sports channel.

③ Let's watch *Susie Superspy*. It's on the new movie channel.

④ That's a great idea.

⑤ Let's watch that new talk show *Everyone Speaks Out*.

⑥ No, I'd rather watch music videos.

2. **Describe the picture.**

Listen and repeat. Role-play.

 Listen. Sing or chant.

Song

I'd Rather Watch TV

Come on, let's go fishing.
It's such a beautiful day!
And let's go swimming, too.
Tell me, what do you say?
Why not have a picnic
  under skies so blue!
What do you mean you can't?
What is wrong with you?

Oh, I know you are a friend.
I know you think of me.
But never will I miss a chance
* to sit and watch TV.*
First, I watch the news
* and then my favorite show.*
Then cartoons, sports, and talk—
So, sorry, I can't go!

Let's play **soccer**.

5.  **Listen and repeat.**

Let's play **tennis**.
OK.

Let's search **the Internet**.
That's a good idea.

Let's fly **our kites**.
Sorry, I can't.

6. **Write. Use *buy, finish, go, ride,* and *watch*.**

1. _____ to the soccer game.

No, thanks. How about a movie?

2. _____ our homework quickly.

OK.

3. _____ some new shoes.

That's a good idea.

4. _____ a game show on TV.

I want to watch cartoons.

5. _____ our bikes in the park.

I'm too tired.

I'd rather go to the movies.

Listen and repeat.

Let's watch TV. → Sorry, I'd rather ride my bike.
Does Tim want to watch TV? → No, he'd rather read his book.
Will Jill and Jane watch TV? → Oh, they'd rather go to the mall.

B29 Listen and write the number.

1

Write sentences. Look at 8 for ideas.

. Let's walk to the park.

No, thanks. I'd rather watch TV.

2. Let's go hiking.

_____

3. Will you go to the library with me this afternoon?

_____

4. Let's make pizza.

_____

5. Will you play tennis with me later?

_____

6. Let's go skateboarding today.

_____

10. **Listen and repeat.**

I ❤ TV

In my life, I've watched a lot of TV. I love cartoons, so I've seen lots of cartoons. I also love animals, so I've enjoyed many nature shows on TV, too.

Have you watched a lot of TV in your life?	Yes, I have.	No, I haven't.
Has Jerry played lots of video games?	Yes, he has.	No, he hasn't.
Have Jack and Sue done their homework?	Yes, they have.	No, they haven't.

11. **Complete the sentences. Write about yourself.**

been   flown   gone   ~~jumped~~   lived   sung   visited

1. (jump) ___Have___ you ___jumped___ on a trampoline?
   ___Yes, I have.___

2. (fly) _____ you _____ in an airplane?
   _____

3. (visit) _____ you _____ another country?
   _____

4. (be) _____ you _____ to a music concert?
   _____

5. (sing) _____ you _____ in public?
   _____

6. (go) _____ you _____ to a baseball game?
   _____

7. (live) _____ you _____ in another city?
   _____

12. 🔘 **Listen and repeat.**

Have you ever been to a TV studio?
No, I've never been to a TV studio.

Has Kim ever watched the music channel?
Yes, she has often watched it.

Have Bill and Sonia ever seen a game show?
No, they've never seen one.

13. Write. Then ask and answer.

news show

talk show

comedy show

sports show

1. (you / visit / TV studio)   Have you ever visited a TV studio?

No, I've never visited a TV studio.

2. (you / listen / news show) _____

_____

3. (Tim / see / talk show) _____

_____

4. (they / watch /
   comedy show) _____

_____

5. (Ann / see / sports show) _____

_____

6. (you / watch /
   TV in another language) _____

_____

Writing

14. Read.

> **Paragraphs of Opinion**
>
> When you give your opinion about something, you say why you think your ideas are right. In a paragraph of opinion, it is important to show <u>why</u> you think you are right. Support your ideas with detail sentences that help your reader understand why your opinion is correct.

15. Read Jake's first paragraph.

> ### My Favorite Cartoon
> ### by Jake Moser
>
> Have you ever seen the TV show *Duke, the Daring Dog Detective*? It's my favorite TV show. I like this cartoon a lot. Duke is a big, slow dog. He has big floppy ears and big feet. He wags his tail a lot. Have you ever known a dog like Duke? This show is on TV every Saturday morning. I'd rather watch Duke than any other TV program.

Jake tells us that he likes the TV show *Duke, the Daring Dog Detective*. But he doesn't tell us <u>why</u> it is his favorite show. He doesn't support his opinions with reasons. He needs to try again.

16. Read Jake's new paragraph.

> ### My Favorite Cartoon
> ### by Jake Moser
>
> Have you ever seen the TV show *Duke, the Daring Dog Detective*? It's my favorite TV show. I'd rather watch this show than any other TV show. Duke's adventures are interesting and funny. He gets into some exciting and silly situations, but he always catches the bad guys. Duke is sometimes afraid, but he does the right thing. The artist who draws Duke is very good. Duke looks like a real dog, not a cartoon. When you are watching him, you forget that he isn't a real dog! I really love *Duke, the Daring Dog Detective*.

17. Read Jake's new paragraph again. Underline the detail sentences that tell us <u>why</u> *Duke* is his favorite show.

Writing

18. **Write the name of a TV show you like on the TV screen. Then list the things you like about the show.**

_____

_____

_____

_____

_____

_____

_____

19. **Write a paragraph about your TV show. Use your list of details, and use Jake's new paragraph as a model.**

20. **Work with a partner. Identify the opinion and the details that support the opinion in your partner's paragraph.**

Game Time

21. Play and say.

Have you ever made cookies? No, I've never made cookies.

2. Read and discuss.

Try New Things

Don't be afraid to try new things. Some new things you will like.

Having new skills and experiences makes you more interesting.

3. Discuss the questions. Write.

. Why is it important to try new things?

_____

. What are some new things you have tried?

_____

Hobbies Are Fun

1. **Listen and repeat.**

2. **Describe the picture.**

B33 Listen and repeat. Role-play.

① So that's your hobby. It looks like fun.

② Yeah. I love building things. It's really great.

③ And sewing is my hobby. What about you, Ann?

⑤ Oh, come on. Everyone likes to do something.

④ I don't have time for a hobby.

⑥ I'd rather read than do anything else.

B34 Listen. Sing or chant.

Song

No Time for a Hobby

Everybody I know has a hobby,
  everybody but me.
I don't have time for a hobby.
I'm very busy, you see.
Some people take up sewing.
Some people swim in the sea.
Some people go cave exploring,
  but that will never be me.

Some people like flying kites.
Some people try keeping bees.
Some people love coin collecting,
  but that will never be me.
Everybody I know has a hobby,
  everybody but me.
I don't have time for a hobby.
I'm very busy, you see.

Hobbies Are Fun 101

5. B35 **Listen and repeat.**

What do you think?

Swimming is good exercise.
Hiking is interesting.
Playing tennis is hard.

Drawing is fun.
Collecting coins is great.
Sewing is boring.

6. **What do you think about each activity? Ask and answer.**

boring   confusing   exciting   fun   great   hard   interesting   silly

1 sew clothes

2 collect shells

3 play chess

4 cook

5 build models

6 dance

7. Look at 6. Express your opinion.

1. _Sewing clothes is hard._ _____

2. _____

3. _____

4. _____

5. _____

6. _____

I like swimming.

8. B36 **Listen and repeat.**

> I like rowing my boat.
> They enjoy playing video games.
> He's interested in building model airplanes.

9. B37 💬 **Listen and check rows 1–4. Then ask a friend and check row 5.**

What does Alice like doing?

She enjoys taking photos and reading.

	📷	🛹	♟	🧵	🪙	📚
1. Alice	✓					✓
2. Bobby						
3. Yuriko						
4. Carmen						
5. _____						

10. Look at 9. Write.

1. Alice _enjoys taking photos and reading_____.

2. Bobby _____.

3. Bobby and Yuriko _____.

4. Carmen and Alice _____.

5. _____.
   (my friend)

11. What do you like doing? Write.

_____

Learn and Practice

12. Complete the conversations.

1. Have you ever explored a cave?

No, I haven't. I think exploring caves is dangerous.
(no / dangerous)

2. Have you ever gone on a roller coaster?

_____
(yes / exciting)

3. Have you ever knitted a sweater?

_____
(no / hard)

4. Have you ever played table tennis?

_____
(yes / fun)

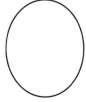

5. Have _____?

_____

you

a friend

How long **have you played soccer?**

Listen and repeat.

> Have you ever collected stamps?
> > Yes, I have. It's fun.
> How long **have you collected stamps?**
> > I've collected stamps for three years.
> How long **has David collected stamps?**
> > For two months.

4. **Ask and answer.**

How long have you played soccer?

For four years. I love playing soccer!

. you / play soccer   for four years
2. she / play guitar   for six months
3. they / build model ships   for a year
. he / take photos   for two months
. he / collect coins   for a month
. they / explore caves   for two years
. she / make jewelry   for six weeks
. you / play chess   for three years

5. **Write.**

. (you / three weeks)
> How long have you taken piano lessons?
> I've taken piano lessons for three weeks.

2. (she / two years)

3. (you / four months)

. (they / five years)

Hobbies Are Fun 105

Writing

16. Read.

> ### The Persuasive Paragraph
> **When you want people to think the same way you do about something, it is important to give them good reasons. In a persuasive paragraph, you list good reasons that persuade your readers to agree with you.**
>> Chess teaches you to think clearly.
>> It also helps you learn to plan ahead.
>
> **Begin and end your paragraph with sentences that influence your readers.**
>> Chess is a wonderful hobby.   (beginning)
>> So if you want a great hobby, try playing chess.   (end)

17. Read Jordi's paragraph.

Coin Collecting
by Jordi Pons

Everyone should have a hobby, and coin collecting is one of the most interesting hobbies of all. There are several reasons why coin collecting is a great hobby. First, coins are part of the history of the world. Collecting them helps you learn about the countries they come from. Second, coins are made of different metals and have interesting designs. Third, coins are fun to trade with other collectors. Finally, some old coins are worth a lot of money. Finding a valuable coin is every collector's dream. Try coin collecting as a hobby. You will learn a lot and have fun at the same time.

18. Write Jordi's reasons for coin collecting in the chart.

Why Coin Collecting Is a Great Hobby
1.
2.
3.
4.

19. Choose a hobby to write about. List some good reasons people should choose this hobby.

_____

_____

_____

_____

_____

20. Write a persuasive paragraph. Use your list of reasons and Jordi's paragraph as a model.

_____
title

by _____

_____

_____

_____

_____

_____

_____

_____

_____

_____

**21. Work with a partner. Identify supporting reasons in your paragraphs.
Are they persuasive?**

22. **Play and say.**

Have you ever built model planes?

How long have you built model planes?

Yes, I have.

For about two years.
I love building models!

23. 💬 **Read and discuss.**

Have a Hobby

Hobbies are educational as well as entertaining.

Hobbies can help you make new friends.

24. 💬 **Discuss the questions. Write.**

1. What are some educational hobbies?

_____

2. How can hobbies help you meet people?

_____

Collecting Stamps

How can you learn about the world without traveling very far? You could start collecting stamps. The first step is deciding what kinds of stamps you are interested in. Would you like to collect stamps from just one country? Is there a special theme, such as animals or space, that interests you? Some people even collect stamps of just one color or shape. It's your choice.

One great thing about stamp collecting is that it's easy to get started. Look at the stamps that come into your own home. Could any of them be what you are looking for? You can also ask relatives and friends to save stamps for you. Then you can find other stamp collectors and trade with them. You can buy new stamps at the post office, or you can go to stamp dealers for older, harder-to-find stamps.

**Some people collect stamps
that match their interests.**

A magnifying glass is used to examine the details on this stamp.

As a stamp collector, you don't need a lot of expensive equipment. All you need is a stamp album and some hinges or mounts to hold your stamps in place. (Don't tape or glue your stamps to the page. When you try to remove them, they may tear.) You will also need some tongs to handle the stamps because your fingers can damage them. Finally, you need a magnifying glass to help you see small differences between similar stamps.

From a small start, you can build a stamp collection that will be a source of pleasure, knowledge, and maybe even money in the years to come!